First World War
and Army of Occupation
War Diary
France, Belgium and Germany

16 DIVISION
Divisional Troops
Divisional Trench Mortar Batteries
1 June 1916 - 21 August 1916

WO95/1963/3-4

The Naval & Military Press Ltd
www.nmarchive.com
Published in association with The National Archives

Published by

The Naval & Military Press Ltd

Unit 10 Ridgewood Industrial Park,

Uckfield, East Sussex,

TN22 5QE England

Tel: +44 (0) 1825 749494

www.naval-military-press.com

www.nmarchive.com

This diary has been reprinted in facsimile from the original. Any imperfections are inevitably reproduced and the quality may fall short of modern type and cartographic standards.

© Crown Copyright
Images reproduced by permission of The National Archives, London, England, 2015.

Contents

Document type	Place/Title	Date From	Date To
Heading	WO95/1963/3		
Heading	War Diary X16. Y16, Z16 Trench Mortar Batters 1st. July to 31st. July 1916 Volume No. 3		
War Diary	Loos Sector	01/07/1916	01/07/1916
War Diary	14 Bis.	01/07/1916	01/07/1916
War Diary	Loos Sector	02/07/1916	02/07/1916
War Diary	14 Bis	02/07/1916	02/07/1916
War Diary	Loos Sector	03/07/1916	03/07/1916
War Diary	14 Bis	03/07/1916	03/07/1916
War Diary	Loos Sector	04/07/1916	04/07/1916
War Diary	14 Bis	04/07/1916	04/07/1916
War Diary	Loos Sector	05/07/1916	05/07/1916
War Diary	14 Bis	05/07/1916	05/07/1916
War Diary	Loos Sector	06/07/1916	06/07/1916
War Diary	14 Bis	06/07/1916	06/07/1916
War Diary	Loos Sector	07/07/1916	07/07/1916
War Diary	14. Bis.	07/07/1916	07/07/1916
War Diary	Loos. Sector	08/07/1916	08/07/1916
War Diary	14 Bis	08/07/1916	08/07/1916
War Diary	Loos Sector	09/07/1916	09/07/1916
War Diary	14 Bis	09/07/1916	09/07/1916
War Diary	Loos Sector	10/07/1916	10/07/1916
War Diary	14 Bis	10/07/1916	10/07/1916
War Diary	Loos. Sector	11/07/1916	11/07/1916
War Diary	14 Bis	11/07/1916	11/07/1916
War Diary	Loos Sector	12/07/1916	12/07/1916
War Diary	14 Bis	12/07/1916	12/07/1916
War Diary	Loos. Sector	13/07/1916	13/07/1916
War Diary	14 Bis	13/07/1916	13/07/1916
War Diary	Loos.	15/07/1916	15/07/1916
War Diary	14 Bis	15/07/1916	15/07/1916
War Diary	X 16.	15/07/1916	15/07/1916
War Diary	Loos	16/07/1916	16/07/1916
War Diary	14 Bis.	16/07/1916	16/07/1916
War Diary	Loos.	17/07/1916	17/07/1916
War Diary	14 Bis	17/07/1916	17/07/1916
War Diary	Loos.	18/07/1916	18/07/1916
War Diary	14 Bis.	18/07/1916	18/07/1916
War Diary	Loos	19/07/1916	19/07/1916
War Diary	14 Bis	19/07/1916	19/07/1916
War Diary	Loos.	20/07/1916	20/07/1916
War Diary	14 Bis.	20/07/1916	20/07/1916
War Diary	Loos.	21/07/1916	21/07/1916
War Diary	14 Bis.	21/07/1916	21/07/1916
War Diary	Loos.	22/07/1916	22/07/1916
War Diary	14 Bis	22/07/1916	22/07/1916
War Diary	Loos	23/07/1916	23/07/1916
War Diary	14 Bis	23/07/1916	23/07/1916
War Diary	Quarry Sector	24/07/1916	24/07/1916
War Diary	14 Bis	24/07/1916	24/07/1916

War Diary	Quarry Sector	25/07/1916	25/07/1916
War Diary	14 Bis.	25/07/1916	25/07/1916
War Diary	Quarry Sector	26/07/1916	26/07/1916
War Diary	14 Bis	26/07/1916	26/07/1916
War Diary	Quarry Sector	27/07/1916	27/07/1916
War Diary	14 Bis	27/07/1916	27/07/1916
War Diary	Quarries Sector	28/07/1916	28/07/1916
War Diary	14 Bis	28/07/1916	28/07/1916
War Diary	Quarries Sector	29/07/1916	29/07/1916
War Diary	14 Bis	29/07/1916	29/07/1916
War Diary	Quarries Sector	30/07/1916	30/07/1916
War Diary	14 Bis	30/07/1916	30/07/1916
War Diary	Quarries Sector	31/07/1916	31/07/1916
War Diary	14 Bis	31/07/1916	31/07/1916
Heading	War Diary 47th Light Trench Mortar Battery 1st. July To 31st. July 1916 Volume No. 3		
War Diary	Noeux-Les Mines	01/06/1916	01/06/1916
War Diary	Loos Sector (Right)	26/06/1916	27/07/1916
Heading	War Diary 48th Light Trench Mortar Battery 1st. July to 31st July 1916 Volume No.		
War Diary	14 Bis	01/07/1916	12/07/1916
War Diary	Noeux Les Mines	13/07/1916	20/07/1916
War Diary	Loos	20/07/1916	22/07/1916
War Diary	Maguirgabe	23/07/1916	24/07/1916
War Diary	Huilverd	25/07/1916	31/07/1916
War Diary	Aldershot.	31/07/1916	31/07/1916
War Diary	Folkestone	01/08/1916	01/08/1916
War Diary	Boulogne	02/08/1916	08/08/1916
War Diary	Lebrewil Bucamp	15/08/1916	21/08/1916
Heading	WO95/1963/4		
Heading	16th Division Trench Mortar Batteries. Jly 1916-1918 Sept. 1919 Jan		
War Diary	Bucamp.	01/09/1918	01/09/1918
War Diary	Ruitz	02/09/1918	30/09/1918
War Diary	Alicay	02/10/1918	04/10/1918
War Diary	Bercleau	05/10/1918	12/10/1918
War Diary	Cambrin Bercleau	12/10/1918	15/10/1918
War Diary	Cambrin	16/10/1918	16/10/1918
War Diary	Haisnes	17/10/1918	17/10/1918
War Diary	Douvrin	18/10/1918	18/10/1918
War Diary	Provin	19/10/1918	19/10/1918
War Diary	Attiches	20/10/1918	20/10/1918
War Diary	Templeuve	21/10/1918	21/10/1918
War Diary	La Posterie	22/10/1918	22/10/1918
War Diary	Rumes	23/10/1918	24/10/1918
War Diary	Merlin	28/10/1918	30/10/1918
War Diary	Merlin	01/11/1918	10/11/1918
War Diary	Rumes	11/11/1918	11/11/1918
War Diary	Merlin	14/11/1918	14/11/1918
War Diary	Rumes	15/11/1918	15/11/1918
War Diary	Pont-A-Marcq	16/11/1918	16/11/1918
War Diary	Libercourt	17/11/1918	27/11/1918
War Diary	Libercourt.	06/01/1919	28/01/1919

Woas/1963/3

W A R   D I A R Y

X 16., Y 16, Z 16
Trench Mortar Batteries

1st. July to 31st. July 1916.

VOLUME No. 3.

16
X.Y.Z. 16.
M.T.M. Batteries
Vol 1
Trench Mortars

Jy '16
Jan 19

16
July

X.Y & 7L Batteries Army Form C. 2118.
16th Division Medium Trench Mortars

WAR DIARY
or
INTELLIGENCE SUMMARY.
(Erase heading not required.)

Place	Date	Hour	Summary of Events and Information	Remarks and references to Appendices
Loos Sector	1/4/16	Y&X	Shelled enemy Front-line M.6 & O.32. Good effect. The enemy returned very heavy No of rounds fired 21	
14 Bee.	1/4/16	Y&X	Shelled enemy Front-line H.35.d.5.5.8. H.25.d.10. Good effect. Enemy retaliated Moderately. No of rounds fired 15	
Loos Sector	2/4/16	Y&X	Fired behind Hohenzollern Redoubt with a observation to enemy of repair work. No of rounds fired 34	
14 Bee	2/4/16	Y&X	Fired on M.G. Emplacement which was destroyed also a M.M. Trench. No of rounds fired 25.	
Loos Sector	3/4/16	Y&X	Fired on Hearts Redoubt Sap-heads & support line opposite M.5.7.M.5.5. No of rounds fired 47	
14 Bee	3/4/16	Y&X	Shelled enemy Front line at H.25.b.5.5. H.31.b.1.5. H.26.t.9.7 H.31.6.1.7 considerable damage done to enemy's front line & wire. No of rounds.	
			Winds. E.	
Loos Sector	4/4/16	Y&X	Shelled enemy wire at M.5.d.7.5. effect good. Enemy did not retaliate. No of rounds fired. 25.	

WAR DIARY
or
INTELLIGENCE SUMMARY.
(Erase heading not required.)

Army Form C. 2118.

Place	Date	Hour	Summary of Events and Information	Remarks and references to Appendices
Bu	4/11/16	2.9 x	Shelled enemy's front line at H25d 6.2, H25.b.5.5. Good results. 9 rds fired 22	
Trenches	5/11/16	7.9 x	Fired at intervals on enemy at M.5.d.7½.4½ & M6.C.1.2. Effect poor owing to difficulty in observing n.° of Rds fired 30.	
14 Bu	5/11/16	2.9 x	Fired on front line in Bn Sub Sector H.35.b.5.1.3.9. 40 Rds were during the day. N° of rounds fired 19.	
Loos Junction	6/11/16	7.12 x	Fired 35 rds on wire at M.6.c.1.5.2. Excellent results. Fired at selected points Enemy retaliated with Trench Mortars	
14 Bu	6/11/16	2.9 x	Fired on selected points. Effect Good 90 Rds fired 50.	
Loos Sector	7/11/16	7.9 x	Fired on enemy front line at M.5.d.1.1.1, M.5.6.3.5, M.6.C.9.5 & M.6.C.9.5. 200 rounds fired 67.8 Effect good. Enemy retaliated with small Mortars. Shrapnel Proposed. One Corporal Killed. 9 Ore.	
14 Bu	7/11/16	2.2 x	3 rds on H.25.b.5.5. N.W.W. good Infantry ordered 20 rds firing of Bombardment at Battn in Marylebone 11.15 pm	
Loos Sector	8/11/16	1.1 x	Fired 43 rds on selected points. 1m & J.P. Guns. No Retaliation	
14 Bu	8/11/16	2.9 x	150 rds fired at selected points. Result Good	

WAR DIARY or INTELLIGENCE SUMMARY

(Erase heading not required.)

Army Form C. 2118.

Place	Date	Hour	Summary of Events and Information	Remarks and references to Appendices
Loos Sect.	9/4/16	4½x	115 rd.a.f.n.g. on enemy's trenches sw. at SW.Lens Rd Pauls Rd & trolley route W.	
1st Bde	9/7/16	7.9.3.x	All rds on front line at H.11.b.1.9 & H.25.b.9.2	
Loos Sector	10/1/16	4½x	40 rds. ong. the enemy's wire	
1st Bde	10/1/16	2½x	43 rds on f.a.f.s in enemy wire. Sharp retaliation by 5.9 & 4.2	
Loos Sector	11/7/16	4½x	150 rds on front defences A to B. Alleyand at M.5.d.5x, M.5.d.7x.4.3 & M.6.d.5.5½.	
			Enemy retaliated serv. heavy on Hwe. village	
1st Bde	11/7/16	7.9.2.x	80 rds fired at H.25.b. 5.5./ H.25.c.0.1½. H.25.b.9.9 H.25.b.3.3 Very effective	
Loos Sector	12/7/16	4½x	100 rds a lot M.5.d.8.5½. M.5.d.7x.4.5 M.6.b.½.5½ Good results. Heavy retaliation	
			1 man wounded	
1st Bde	12/7/16	2½x	10 rds at H.25.b.4.7 H.25.b.5.5. H.25.d.0.1½ H.25.d.3.3 Result Good Enemy	
			Retaliated very heavily. 1 man wounded + 1 gun out of action	
Loos Sector	13/7/16	4½x	10 rds fired on trenches at N.31.1. M.5.7. M.5.d.7½.4.5 M.6.b.5½	
			& H.25.b	
1st Bde	13/7/16	7.9.x	& 7 rds fired on trenches opposite Bryan 62 also opp.opposite	
			Boyeau 62.9 front line at H.a.5.b.5.5 H.25.b.1½.1½/	

WAR DIARY
or
INTELLIGENCE SUMMARY.

Army Form C. 2118.

(Erase heading not required.)

Instructions regarding War Diaries and Intelligence Summaries are contained in F.S. Regs., Part II. and the Staff Manual respectively. Title pages will be prepared in manuscript.

Place	Date	Hour	Summary of Events and Information	Remarks and references to Appendices
L.00.	15/7/16	Y16	52 rds on Enemy's front line. Trenches very badly damaged.	
1A 18.10.	15/7/16	Z16	38 rds on Enemy Support line. Doing great damage to trenches and workings.	
X.16.	15/7/16		Attached to 61" Div.	
L.00.	16/7/16	Y16	11 rds on Enemy's front & Support line. Effective.	
1A 18.10.	16/7/16	Z16	10 rds on Enemy's dump at H.5.b.8.5.a. Good.	
L.00.	17/7/16	Y16	30 rds at trenches near M.5.d.6.3. M.5.d.9.4½. M.6.B.3.5½. & behind Seaforth bridge & Hectorwood.	
1A 18.10	17/7/16	Z16	50 rds on Lt Mortar at H.25.b.9.1½. Dugout at H.25.d.4.0. M.t Hilliet H.25.d.3.2. Great damage done to trenches & dugouts, from hit & further thrown in. All the Enemy retaliation 5-9	
L.00.	18/7/16	Y16	23 rds on aeroplane 5 direct hits, machine reduced to a wreckage. 10 rds Seaforth Bridge. Heavy Retaliation	
1A 18.10	18/7/16	Z16	20 rds on communication trench. Considerable material thrown up. Enemy Trench Mortar silenced	

Army Form C. 2118.

WAR DIARY
or
INTELLIGENCE SUMMARY.
(Erase heading not required.)

Instructions regarding War Diaries and Intelligence Summaries are contained in F. S. Regs., Part II. and the Staff Manual respectively. Title pages will be prepared in manuscript.

Place	Date	Hour	Summary of Events and Information	Remarks and references to Appendices
L.O.O.	19/7/16	Y/16	25 rds. In area of M.6.0.9.9. Harass on Crater. In retaliation to enemy grenades + Shell fire.	
1/A Bio	19/7/16	Y/16	4 rds on H.25.d.0.2 + 10 rds. on M.6. Hill. Good effect. Enemy retaliated heavily with 5.9s. Total rds fired 14.	
L.O.O.	20/7/16	Y/16	35 rds. In vicinity of Harrisons + Hartz Crater. Enemy retaliated moderately. 1 Gunner Wounded.	
1/A Bio	20/7/16	Y/16	45 rds on Sap 1 + open Crater. Very Effective.	
L.O.O.	21/7/16	Y/16	39 rds in retaliation to enemy ?.M.B. and rifle fire.	
1/A Bio	21/7/16	Y/16	37 rds fired communication trench at H.31.B.2.6. + Various points. In retaliation to enemy fire.	
L.O.O.	22/7/16	Y/16	90 rounds fire changing sector.	
1/A Bio	22/7/16	Y/16	10 rds fired at various points. Amm reserved for a night operation.	
L.O.O.	23/7/16	Y/16	Relief proceeding.	
1/A Bio	23/7/16	Y/16	40 rds fired in retaliation to Enemy T.M. & T.M.C. silenced	

WAR DIARY
or
INTELLIGENCE SUMMARY.
(Erase heading not required.)

Army Form C. 2118.

Place	Date	Hour	Summary of Events and Information	Remarks and references to Appendices
Quarry Sector	24/11/16	Y1 X	37 rds fired in vicinity of G.12.a.4.0 & H.13.a.2.7. Effective. In retaliation to Enemy T.M.s	
14 Bns	24/11/16	X Y X	31 rds fired at bomb H.25.b.4.7½ H.25.b.6.5 H.25.c.0.6½ H.25.d.3.3. In retaliation to Hostile T.M.s	
Quarry Sector	25/11/16	Y9 X	Enemy's front line shelled at G.12.b.3.1.9. H.13.a.2.8. Infantry order to cease fire. Very Effective. Retaliation Heavy in 6.6. Wainga.	
14 Bns	25/11/16	Z Y X	40 rds on pd H.25.d.0 & H.25.d.4.2. Retaliation to enemy T.M.s	
Quarry Sector	26/11/16	Y1 X	50 rds on G.12.a.4.0 G.13.a.2.7 & G.12.b.31. In retaliation to hostile T.M.s	
14 Bns	26/11/16	Z Y X	Fired 20 rds at H.25.b.5.5 H.25.d.0.13 H.25.d.3.3. In retaliation to hostile T.M.s	
Quarry Sector	27/11/16	Y1 X	20 rds on wire at G.12.a.3.1. 40.9.20. 2 a.m. took 4 T.M. in Quarry	
14 Bns	27/11/16	Z Y X	37 rds on wire and parapet at H.31.b/2.5. H.25.b.33 & H.25.a.9.2. Enemy Retaliation Ineffective	

Army Form C. 2118.

WAR DIARY
or
INTELLIGENCE SUMMARY.
(Erase heading not required.)

Instructions regarding War Diaries and Intelligence Summaries are contained in F. S. Regs, Part II. and the Staff Manual respectively. Title pages will be prepared in manuscript.

Place	Date	Hour	Summary of Events and Information	Remarks and references to Appendices
Quarrie Secto	28/7/16	4.45	No Progress Report Received from the Line	
14 Bis	29/7/16	2.65 am	51 Rounds On Wire and Parapet at H.25.c.54 H.25.d.22 H.31.b.66 Very Effective Enemy Retaliation Normal	
Quarrie Secto	29/7/16	4.52 am	35. On wire at Crater Area about G.11.c.8.4 Good 10 Rounds H.13 a.2.3 Fair line & vicinity Effect Good. Enemy Retaliation Heavy with Rifle Grenades. 2 Gunners Wounded.	
14 Bis		2.63 am	35 Rounds On wire at H.31.b.1.5 H.25.b.1.2 H.25.d.55. Effective. Enemy Retaliation Moderate	
Quarrie Secto	30/7/16	4.55 am	44 Rounds On wire 9 front line opposite G.18.5 G.12.6 G.12.a.50 G.11.1 Very Effective Enemy Retaliation Moderate	
14 Bis	30/7/16	2.63 am	35 Rounds front line 9 wire at H.31.b.12.4 H.31 & 0.97 Rifle Wire at H.25.d.o. Effective Enemy Retaliation Moderate	

Army Form C. 2118.

WAR DIARY
or
INTELLIGENCE SUMMARY.
(Erase heading not required.)

Place	Date	Hour	Summary of Events and Information	Remarks and references to Appendices
Gravois Secton	30/6/16	Y62M6	23 Rounds on front & support trench opposite G18.s Effective Enemy Retaliation Slight	
14 Bio	30/7/16	Z16.N6	10 Rounds on Minenfield Good Effect. In Retaliation 16 Koalils the 22 Rounds on Wire & Front line at H31 L09 & H31.8.4.4 Enemy Retaliation Moderate. 1 Gunner Wounded shell shock	

Lt Col
D.A.A.

WAR DIARY

47th Light Trench
Mortar Battery

1st. July to 31st. July 1916.

VOLUME No. 3.

Army Form C. 2118.

WAR DIARY
or
INTELLIGENCE SUMMARY.
(Erase heading not required.)

47th Trench Mortar Battery

Place	Date	Hour	Summary of Events and Information	Remarks and references to Appendices
NOEUX-LES MINES.			**JUNE**	
			The 47th Trench Mortar Battery was formed on 11.6.16. Personnel & officers, 46 other ranks at Noeux-les-Mines from 11th to 16th June. Leaving reserve personnel of similar strength, the officers & which accompanied the Battery into the line in the Loos sector on 16.6.16. The Battery devised a new system of carrying Stokes ammunition into the line prepared for firing and stock it in bombproof bombproof stores built and placed in position by the 47th Infy Bde workshops.	
LOOS sector (Right) 26/27th			Lt F.J. BIGGANE, 8th Royal Irish Fus: (att'd to mortar bty) slightly wounded right. Battery cooperated with the Artillery in establishing a barrage on either flank of the raiding party of the 7th Leinsters, and was congratulated by the O.C. batt'n upon its effectiveness	
			Casualties during June. 1 Officer wounded (as above), 1 o.r. killed, 1 o.r. wded	

Army Form C. 2118.

WAR DIARY
or
INTELLIGENCE SUMMARY.
(Erase heading not required.)

47th Trench Mortar Battery

Place	Date	Hour	Summary of Events and Information	Remarks and references to Appendices
			JULY	
	2.7.16		Relieved by 49th T.M.B., returned to NOEUX-LES-MINES, again training Reserve personnel and replacing casualties	
	16.7.16		Relieved 48th T.M.B. in PUITS 14 BIS Sector.	
	18/19th	Night	Cooperated with Artillery during attempted raid by 8th R.M.F.	
	19/20 th	Night	Cooperated with Artillery during another raid by same batt'n	
	22/23rd	Night	Cooperated with Artillery during raid by 6th R. Irish Regt.	
	28/29 th	Night	Cooperated with Artillery during raid by 8th R.M.F.	
	29/30 th	Night	Cooperated with Artillery during another raid by same batt'n	
	30.7.16		Relieved by 49th T.M.B. Returned to NOEUX-LES-MINES.	
	27.7.16		A defective shell burst in the bore of a STOKES 3" gun, severely wounding one man. During this period our fire had a marked effect upon hostile grenade and aerial dart fire, over which, towards the end of the period, we showed marked superiority. We were not however so successful in our attempts to silence hostile minenwerfer, to which however we invariably replied. It was discovered that one of the new types of cartridge issued	

Army Form C. 2118.

47ᵗʰ Trench Mortar Battery

WAR DIARY
or
INTELLIGENCE SUMMARY.
(Erase heading not required.)

Place	Date	Hour	Summary of Events and Information	Remarks and references to Appendices
			JULY (Cont'd)	
			was defective, and a report on the matter was duly forwarded.	
			Casualties during July. 2 O.R. killed, 4 O.R. wounded.	
			E.R. Law 2/Lt a/o.c 47ᵗʰ T.M.B	

WAR DIARY

48th Light Trench Mortar Battery

1st. July to 31st. July 1916.

VOLUME No.

WAR DIARY
or
INTELLIGENCE SUMMARY.

Army Form C. 2118.

48th Inf. Bde.
48th Light T.M. Battery

(Erase heading not required.)

Place	Date	Hour	Summary of Events and Information	Remarks and references to Appendices
	July 1916			

Army Form C. 2118.

WAR DIARY
or
INTELLIGENCE SUMMARY.
(Erase heading not required.)

Instructions regarding War Diaries and Intelligence Summaries are contained in F. S. Regs., Part II. and the Staff Manual respectively. Title pages will be prepared in manuscript.

Place	Date	Hour	Summary of Events and Information	Remarks and references to Appendices
Noeux	18		On Divisional Reserve	
			Battery manned by [illegible] [illegible] to Bde H.Q.	
Nœux	20		Guns cleaned & officers & N.C.O. Discussed. All equipment inspected & essentials improved.	
			6.N.O. for Major to Second division.	
			Battery moved up to Magnicourt in readiness to relief 148 Bryde. Div now in Ist Corps.	
			Wounded by enemy shell T. [illegible] [illegible]	
		21		
Nœux	22		Major & [illegible] Division with [illegible] leaves for [illegible] days	
			Arthur not here. Men enjoying magnificent weather & full sized dinner. Busy with organization and further Mess kits & necessary	
			Easter day and Sister Mess even Nicolaes	
			Major 148 Bde enquires need	
Magnicourt	23		In Reserve at Magnicourt. Cavalry ???	
		24			

Army Form C. 2118.

WAR DIARY
or
INTELLIGENCE SUMMARY.
(Erase heading not required.)

Instructions regarding War Diaries and Intelligence Summaries are contained in F. S. Regs., Part II. and the Staff Manual respectively. Title pages will be prepared in manuscript.

Place	Date	Hour	Summary of Events and Information	Remarks and references to Appendices
Millsand	23		[illegible handwritten entries]	
	h			
	31			

29-9

16 D T M Bty

Army Form C. 2118.

WAR DIARY
or
INTELLIGENCE SUMMARY.
(Erase heading not required.)

of 3

Place	Date	Hour	Summary of Events and Information	Remarks and references to Appendices
ALDERSHOT	31st July	11.0 am	16th Div. T.M. Brigade 6" Newton Medium Entrained for FOLKESTONE.	
FOLKESTONE	1 Augt	2.6 am	Left FOLKESTONE Embarked BOULOGNE Arrived BOULOGNE Rest Camp.	
BOULOGNE	2 Augt	9 am	Entrained Div Area SAMER. Billeted at LE BREUIL.	
	3 Augt		X Battery proceeded 1st Army School of Mortars.	
LE BREUIL (Bu Camp.	6 Augt		Y Battery proceeded 1st Army School of Mortars. X Battery returned to LE BREUIL	
	21 Augt		X Battery joined 1st Army School and Batteries continued training there till 31st Augt.	

Brigade was formed at BOURLEY CAMP, ALDERSHOT, after mobilization following officers proceeded overseas

D.T.M.O.   Capt. J. S. Whitehead   R.F.A.

X Battery.
Capt. W. J. Hoophunter   R.F.A.
(revealitated 16th Div Arty.

Y Battery.
Lieut. C.W. Hartnoll   R.F.A.   2/Lt of Capt. CH Clarke   R.F.A.
2/Lt   Cpl. Hawson   R.F.A.   2/Lt   B Hall   R.F.A.
2/Lt   J.A. Gregory R.F.A.   2/Lt   L Hodgson R.F.A.
                                     2/Lt   J.S. Wyborn R.F.A.

Other ranks 52 of which 47 were   Other ranks 53 men of which 47 were
Category B1.   Category B1.

D.T.M.O.
16 D.T.M. Bty.

moas/1963/4

16TH DIVISION

TRENCH MORTAR BATTERIES.

JLY 1916 - ~~JAN 1919~~

1918 SEPT - 1919 JAN

Army Form C. 2118.

WAR DIARY
or
INTELLIGENCE SUMMARY.
(Erase heading not required.)

Instructions regarding War Diaries and Intelligence Summaries are contained in F.S. Regs., Part II. and the Staff Manual respectively. Title pages will be prepared in manuscript.

16 D T M Bay

Place	Date	Hour	Summary of Events and Information	Remarks and references to Appendices
BUCAMP	1918 1 Sept	2 p.m.	X and Y Batteries proceeded from ARMY SCHOOL to RUITZ to join Division.	
RUITZ	2 Sept	6 p.m.	X and Y Batteries took over the French Mortars on Divisional Front from 1st Division Batteries X and Y. Divisional Front extended from LA BASSEE CANAL on the NORTH to approximately a line due EAST along SOUTHERLY Gridlines of G4 and G5 Ref. map GORRE 2nd Edition 1/20,000.	
	10 Sept		Ordinary trench warfare was carried on till 9th September. The enemy started withdrawing leaving all positions out of range. Steps were at once taken to push Mortars forward and two sections mobilised for open warfare. No opportunity offered however as the enemy only withdrew a short distance and the enormous mine craters formed gave much of an obstacle for wheeled transport. Guns were however got up by hand.	
	22 Sept		15th Div on our right and 55th Div on our left took over part of 16th Divisional Line and all positions both forward and defensive in these areas were handed over.	
	23 Sept		Y/16 Battery were with two mobile special beds. One was tried on 24th with good results.	
	26 to 30 Sept		Wire cutting on the HAINES - HULLUCH LINE was carried out.	

[signature] Capt. R.F.A.
D.T.M.O. 16th Division.

Sheet 1

Army Form C. 2118.

SECRET.

WAR DIARY
INTELLIGENCE SUMMARY.
(Erase heading not required.)

D.T.M.O. 1- NOV 1918 16TH DIVISION

19th vol 5

Place	Date	Hour	Summary of Events and Information	Remarks and references to Appendices
AUCHY	Oct 1918 2nd	1500	O.C. T.M.O. and O/c the T.M.B. reconnoitred as far as HAISNES on retirement of enemy	
"	3rd 4th	From 1430	O/c T.M.O. and I/c B. I/c reconnoitred possible positions behind BILLY BERCLEAU Ist officer and 17 OR's sent to DOUVRIN with two Mobile Howitzers to take up close position with Battalion commanders and to be ready for action if called upon	
BERCLEAU	5th	1500	One Mobile T.M fired from BERCLEAU on LAFERME Triangulaire shell fell in road and canal Shoot very successful - 20 rounds fired.	
	6th-7th		92 rounds fired from Triangulaire on B.H.Q. Shooting very good and report received that the hit was considered satisfactory	
"	7th	Noon	A/Capt A/W Shadwell and 2nd /Lt Montgomerison also Cpl Riley wounded by enemy T.M's at DYNAMITE FACTORY.	
"	7th	2100	Gunner Shadwell wounded by M.G bullet whilst taking #TM to DYNAMITE FACTORY	
"	9th	1600	40 rounds fired on house C13 c40 b0 - 20 direct hits - Unjust damage done	
"			50 rounds fired on LA FERME C19 à - several direct hits - much damage done	
"	10th	1430	50 rounds fired on LA FERME C19 à - many direct hits	
"		1730	Another Mortar sent to DYNAMITE FACTORY at request of Infantry to be ready to fire on STRONG POINT at C15 c25 66 on the morning of the 11th. It was not considered advisable to fire any more on houses at C13 c40 60 as the remains were practically all concrete and the T.M fuze broke off on impact	
"	11th	Noon	20 rounds fired on houses at C13 c40 60 at the request of Infantry - shooting remarkably accurate. 10 direct hits being observed	
"			40 rounds fired at STRONG POINT C15 c25 40	
"	12th	0900	T.M Reserve billets moved from SALLY LABOURSE to CAMBRIN	

Sheet I

Army Form C. 2118.

WAR DIARY
or
INTELLIGENCE SUMMARY.
(Erase heading not required.)

Instructions regarding War Diaries and Intelligence Summaries are contained in F. S. Regs., Part II. and the Staff Manual respectively. Title pages will be prepared in manuscript.

Place	Date 1918 Oct	Hour	Summary of Events and Information	Remarks and references to Appendices
BERCLEAU	12th	2.30	30 rounds fired on LA FERME at C19 - several direct hits. 1F (A Capt) Horlnow - Hospital	
CAMBRIN	13th	1800 Noon	Two mobile beds received from workshops. One allotted to each Battery	
BERCLEAU			50 rounds on house at C.13 c7 92 and LA FERME - many direct hits and buildings badly knocked about	
"	14th	1115	35 rounds on house C13 c92 - 2 direct hits	
"	15th	1030	4 rounds fired on LA FERME prior to our infantry crossing the HAUTE DEULE CANAL. The enemy having retired, orders were received that all mobile positions were to be withdrawn to CAMBRIN, and that the mobile section was to be kept in readiness	
CAMBRIN	16th	0900	Mobile Section move to BILLY BERCLEAU, with orders to keep in touch with infantry	
		13.30	Brigade moved to HAISNES	
HAISNES	17th	0600	45 R.C.Os and men lent to 16th D.A.C. for duty whilst enemy is retiring	
		1030	Brigade move to DOUVRIN - Mobile Section move to CAMPHIN	
DOUVRIN	18th	0900	Brigade move to PROVIN - Mobile Section move to PONT A MARCQ	
PROVIN	19th	0700	Brigade move to ATTICHES - Mobile Section move to TEMPLEUVE	
ATTICHES	20th	0630	Brigade move to TEMPLEUVE - Mobile Section move to CORBRIEUX	
TEMPLEUVE	21st	0600	Brigade move to LA POSTERIE - Mobile Section move to RUMES	
LA POSTERIE	22nd	0930	Brigade move to RUMES - Mobile Section move (T30 a 50) (RUMES)	
RUMES	23rd	0630	32 N.C.Os and men lent to 180th - 171th Brigade R.F.A. from the men lent to the Divisional Ammunition Column on 17-10-18	
			2 Officers and 2 oRs attached for duty to 16th D.A. to	
			Left W.E Studwicke D.S.T.M.O. attached to 16th Divisional Artillery for duty as Officer - A/Capt C.H.Clark of the Battery took over duties as A/D.S.T.M.O over location Studwicke. Mobile Section move to RUMES T30 a 30	
MERLIN	24th 28th	0900	Mobile Section move to MERLIN L13 c 30 30	
			Mules and men attached to mobile section for transport work withdrawn from forward wagons	

Sheet III
Army Form C. 2118.

WAR DIARY
or
INTELLIGENCE SUMMARY.
(Erase heading not required.)

Place	Date	Hour	Summary of Events and Information	Remarks and references to Appendices
MERLIN	1918 Oct 29th	0900 Evening	Line and attached to D Battery 177th Bde R.F.A. for rations and accommodation. a/a/T.M.O. reconnoitred position for 6" Trench Mortar Guns in Barny Yard at W.18 a.50.70. One 6" M.T. mortar gun placed in position in Barny Yard at W.18 a.50.70 (ZERO LINE o/ gun 75° Grid B)	
	30th	morning	One 6" MT Mortar Gun placed in position at rear of Orchard at V.26 a.45.70 (ZERO LINE o/ gun 30° Grid B)	

[signature]
Capt. R.F.A.
a/D.T.M.O. 16th Division.

SECRET

16 D TM Bty
Vol 6

Army Form C. 2118.

WAR DIARY
or
INTELLIGENCE SUMMARY.
(Erase heading not required.)

Instructions regarding War Diaries and Intelligence Summaries are contained in F. S. Regs., Part II. and the Staff Manual respectively. Title pages will be prepared in manuscript.

Place	Date Nov 1918	Hour	Summary of Events and Information	Remarks and references to Appendices
MERLIN	1st	1.30.	18 rounds fired on occupied Enemy Post at V.20.c.85.15. After the fifth round enemy sniper was seen to run across the open country from the post to V.20.d.00.30. the new battery bed with spades used and shooting very steady	
"	2nd	11.00	6 rounds fired on Enemy strong point at V.20.c.90.20. Enemy movements were observed on roads at V.20.d.10.10	
"	4th	11.00	14 rds fired on left of line at V.20.c.75.20. Gap cut 15 to 20 yards in length	
"	9th	-	The enemy withdrew on the divisional front leaving our guns out of range.	
"	10th	-	Mobile section withdrawn from the line to billets at MERLIN.	
RUMES	11th	11.00	Hostilities ceased from this hour in accordance with the terms of armistice	
MERLIN	14th	-	Mobile Section withdrawn from MERLIN to Bde Headquarters at RUMES.	
RUMES	15th	0930	Brigade moved from RUMES to PONT-A-MARCQ.	
PONT-A-MARCQ	16th	0800	Brigade moved from PONT-MARCQ to LIBERCOURT.	
LIBERCOURT	17th	10.00	General Thanksgiving Service.	
"	19th		Capt Hoskinson R.F. posted to 117th Brigade R.F.A. with effect from this date	
"	25th		Educational Training scheme commenced	
"	27th		A Bde and Bank organised as Royal Artillery Divisional Savings Offices	

_____ Lieut Capt. R.F.A.
D.T.M.O. 16th Division.

30 NOV 1918
16th Divisional Artillery

(50940) W: W4300/P713 750,000 3/18 E 2088 Forms C/2118/5. D. D. & L., London, E.C.

SECRET.

Army Form C. 2118.

WAR DIARY
of
INTELLIGENCE SUMMARY.
(Erase heading not required.)

Instructions regarding War Diaries and Intelligence Summaries are contained in F. S. Regs., Part II and the Staff Manual respectively. Title pages will be prepared in manuscript.

Place	Date	Hour	Summary of Events and Information	Remarks and references to Appendices
LIBERCOURT	1918 Dec 11th		One boatsman sent from the sub-depot for investigation	
"	12th		One boatsman sent from the sub-depot for investigation	
"	25th	1800	Brigade Christmas Dinner and social evening	

Capt. R.F.A.
/ D.T.M.O. 16th Division.

Army Form C. 2118.

WAR DIARY
or
INTELLIGENCE SUMMARY.
(Erase heading not required.)

SECRET

W.D. 8 /16
General

Place	Date	Hour	Summary of Events and Information	Remarks and references to Appendices
IBEZCOURT	1919 JAN'Y 6th	0515	16th (No) INDIAN LABOUR PORTER BRIGADE.	
			2 Men sent to U.K. for demobilization (1 minor + 1 long service)	
	11th		2 do — do — do — do — (1 minor + 1 long service)	
	16th		3 do — do — do — do — (1 long service, 1 guarantee letter, 1 priority group)	
	21st		3 do — do — do — do — (1 over 41 years of age, 1 long service, 1 guarantee letter)	
	28th		7 do — do — do — do — (1 over 41 years of age, 1 long service, 1 shipman, 1 man claimed on AF.S6, 3 priority E cat.)	

[signature]
Capt. R.F.A
D.T.M.O. 16th Division.

www.ingramcontent.com/pod-product-compliance
Lightning Source LLC
Chambersburg PA
CBHW081503160426
43193CB00014B/2577